Zen paths to

Harmony

Zen paths to

Harmony

Journey Editions
Boston • Tokyo • Singapore

Introduction

One of the underlying principles of Zen is concentration on the moment, to experience it exactly as it is in every detail. To achieve this, we must calm the mind, let go of the chatter and allow a stillness to fall. At such a time, we attain clarity of vision, and are able to marvel at the simple things in life that we ordinarily pass over. During the average day, we are swept along by routine, rushing from one thing to the next.

To experience that elusive feeling of harmony we must shed the skin of habitual behavior, which cloaks our senses, and see the world through the eyes of a child. Only then do we notice the wonder of a snowflake, the mystery of a harvest moon hanging full in the sky, or the gentle motion of running water smoothing the surface of a stone.

Life is a gift to be savored—nothing more, nothing less—and the quotations and images chosen for this book have been collected to remind us of this, from the flashes of detail in the three-line haiku of poets such as Basho and Issa, to the wisdom of Mahatma Gandhi, Buddha, and Confucius, and the philosophical thought of Western writers.

By embracing our own true nature and recognizing the cycles of the natural world and our place within it, we can find peace of mind and experience true joy.

From morning,

Perfectly tranquil,

Far removed from

the world's turmoil—

One with the spring mist.

Rengetsu, Buddhist Nun

Flow with whatever may happen

and let your mind be free:

Stay centered by **accepting** whatever you are doing.

This is the ultimate.

Chuang Tzu

Abundant clouds,
A few lingering blossoms,

Fresh summer mountains,

Fragrant green leaves,

And gentle cool breezes.

Rengetsu, Buddhist Nun

I exist as I am,
that is enough.

Walt Whitman

Constant

dripping

hollows out a stone.

Lucretius

If I keep a **green bough** in my heart,

the **singing bird** will come.

Chinese proverb

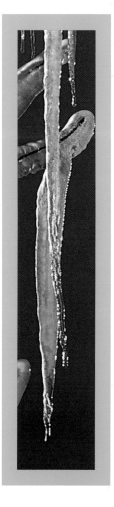

Opening their hearts
ice and **water** become
friends again.

Teishitsu

Lingering

in every pool of water—

spring sunlight.

Issa

Rain bamboos,

wind pines:

all preach **Zen**.

Sayings of the Masters

How delightful—
walking on dewy grasses
in straw sandals.

Haritsu

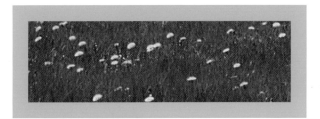

A floating cloud,
Drifting about
Playfully

Here and there

Not wanting to fade away.

Rengetsu, Buddhist Nun

Blue mountains

after rainfall

—much **bluer**.

Sayings of the Masters

I saw it,

but I did not realize it.

Elizabeth Peabody

Water runs

   back to the ocean;

The moon goes down, but

   never leaves the heavens.

Sayings of the Masters

Letting the child

on my back hold some **bracken**

I just picked.

Gyōtai

Evening joy
noontime silence—
spring rain.

Chora

Outside
noisy,
inside empty.

Chinese proverb

My life is an indivisible **whole**,

and all my activities run into one another;

and they have their rise in

my insatiable love of mankind.

Mahatma Gandhi

Everything is in flux.

Heraclitus

Each time the *wind blows*

the butterfly finds a new home

on the willow.

Bashō

The true perfection of man
lies not in what man **has**,
but **in what man is**.

Oscar Wilde

We didn't **inherit the land** from our fathers.
We are borrowing it from our children.

Amish saying

If you want to be happy, be.

Henry David Thoreau

I have often been asked what I thought

was the **secret** of Buddha's **smile**.

It is—it can only be—that he smiles at himself

for **searching** all those years

for what **he already possessed.**

Paul Brunton

Sit

Rest

Work.

Alone with yourself,

Never weary.

On the edge of the forest

Live joyfully,

Without desire.

Buddha

We see men haying far in the meadow,

their heads waving like the grass they cut.

In the distance, the wind seemed to bend all alike.

Henry David Thoreau

The tiny child

shown a **flower**

opens its mouth.

Seifu-jo

The Kingdom of Heaven
is not a place,
but a state of mind.

John Burroughs

The only journey is
the journey within.

Rainer Maria Rilke

It is **essential** that
the **mind** and the **body**
become **motionless**.

Hsier Tao-Kuang

I've scooped the valley's
pine winds for you—

Have a sip!

Sayings of the Masters

I do not know whether I was then a man
dreaming I was a butterfly,
or whether I am now a **butterfly**
dreaming I am a man.

Chuang Tse

Before enlightenment,
I chopped wood and carried water;
after enlightenment,
I chopped wood and carried water.

Zen saying

Eternity is not something that happens after you are dead. It is going on all the time. We are in it now.

Charlotte Perkins Gilman

Watch
fountain murmur!
Hear
mountain color!

Sayings of the Masters

The sense of living is joy enough.

Emily Dickinson

Knock on the sky

And listen to the sound!

Sayings of the Masters

Snow

falls on snow—

silence.

Santōka

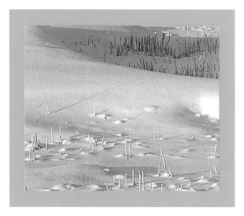

In the fields, in the mountains
    I was **enthralled**, so enthralled;
On the way back home,
    The autumn moon accompanied me
        Right to my room.

Rengetsu, Buddhist Nun

Water originally
contains no **sound**:
Touching a stone
makes it **murmur**.

Sayings of the Masters

Not to care for philosophy

is to be a **true** philosopher.

Blaise Pascal

The **quieter** you become,

the more you can **hear**.

Baba Ram Dass

You will **wake**,
and **remember**,
and
understand.

Robert Browning

First steps on the

Long path to Truth:

Please do not dream

Your lives away,

Walk on to the end.

Rengetsu, Buddhist Nun

Everything *flows*
on and on
like
this river,
without pause,
day and **night**.

Confucius

First published in the United States in 2000 by Journey Editions, an imprint of Periplus Editions (HK) Ltd., with editorial offices at 153 Milk Street, Boston, Massachusetts 02109.

Translations of the poetry of Rengetsu, Buddhist Nun from *Lotus Moon* by John Stevens. Translations of the Sayings of the Masters from *A Zen Forest* by Soiku Shigematsu. Translations of the haiku of Basho, Chora, Gyotai, Haritsu, Issa, Santoka, Seifu-jo, and Teishitsu from *A Haiku Garden* and *Haiku People* by Stephen Addiss. Translations published by permission of Weatherhill, Inc. Photographs of the solitary tree in field, bamboo wind chimes, leaf in the rain, spider's web, and butterfly are reproduced by permission of Neil Sutherland.

Editor: Alison Moss
Series designer: Plum Partnership
Designer: Yvonne Dedman

Library of Congress Catalog Card Number: 00-105135
ISBN: 158290040X

First edition
06 05 04 03 02 01 00 10 9 8 7 6 5 4 3 2 1

Printed in Italy

Distributed by

NORTH AMERICA

Tuttle Publishing
Distribution Center
Airport Industrial Park
364 Innovation Drive
North Clarendon
VT 05759-9436
Tel: (802) 773-8930
Fax: (800) 526-2778

JAPAN

Tuttle Publishing
RK Building, 2nd Floor
2-12-10 Shimo-Meguro
Meguro-Ku
Tokyo 153 0064
Tel: (03) 5437-0171
Fax: (03) 5437-0755

ASIA PACIFIC

Berkeley Books Pte Ltd
5 Little Road 08-01
Singapore 536983
Tel: (65) 280-1330
Fax: (65) 280-6290